AF428220

HOW NOBLE ARE NOBLE GASES?

Chemistry Book for Kids 6th Grade | Children's Chemistry Books

In the Periodic Table of the Elements there is a group of elements called the "noble gases". What are they like? Why do they have that name? Read on and learn more!

Periodic Table

Atomic nomber

Symbol

Name

Atomic Mass

noble gases

2	10	18	36	54	86	118
He	**Ne**	**Ar**	**Kr**	**Xe**	**Rn**	**Uuo**
Helium	Neon	Argon	Krypton	Xenon	Radon	Ununoctium
4.003	20.180	39.948	84.798	131.294	222.018	unknown

EPS 10

WHAT IS A NOBLE GAS?

Being a noble gas is nothing at all like being a king or queen. Hugo Erdmann made up the name "edelgas" in German in 1898 to describe a series of gases scientists were discovering at that time.

One thing these gases have in common is low reactivity, which means they are much less likely to form compounds with other elements. Maybe that does make the noble gases sort of like kings and queens, who have power and have less need of allies than other people do.

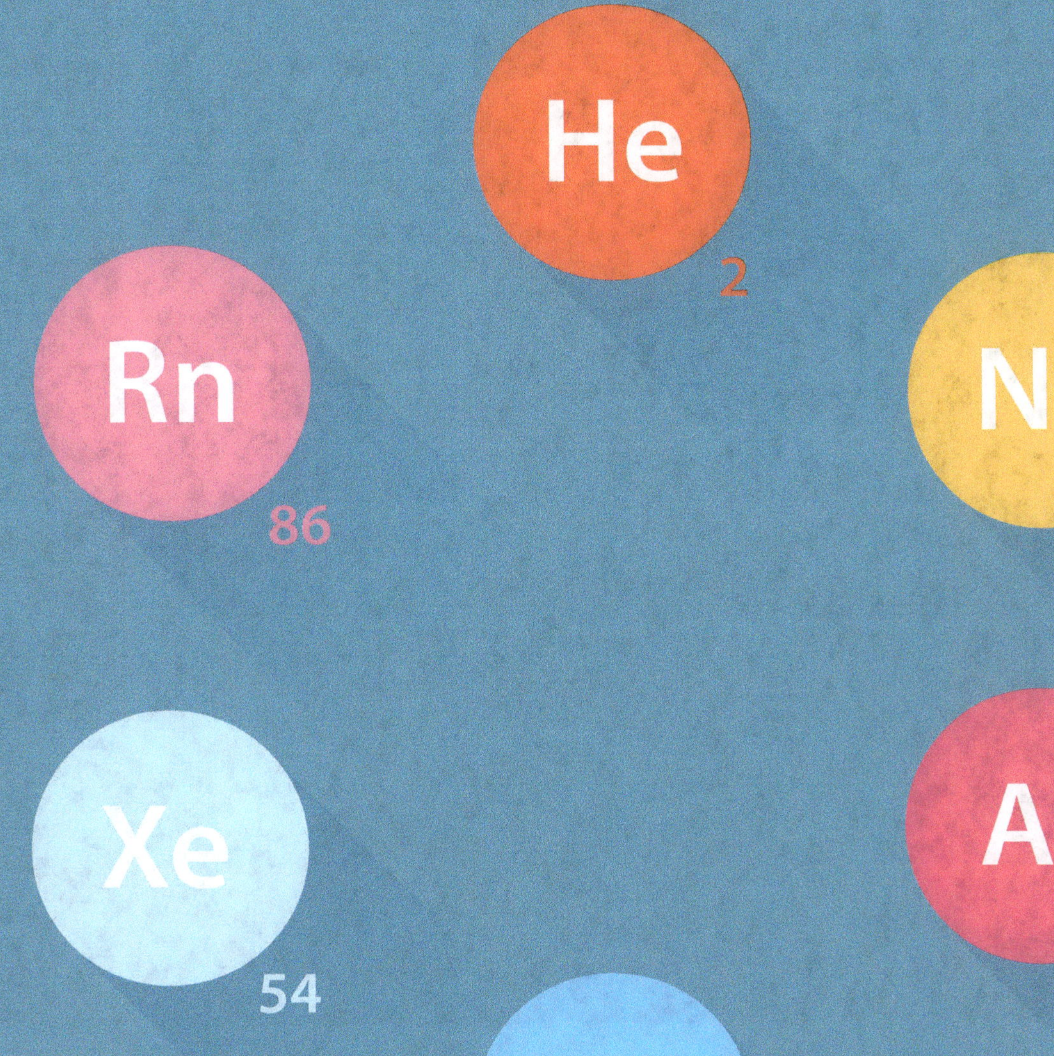

He
2
Rn
86
Ne
10
Xe
54
Ar
18
Kr
36

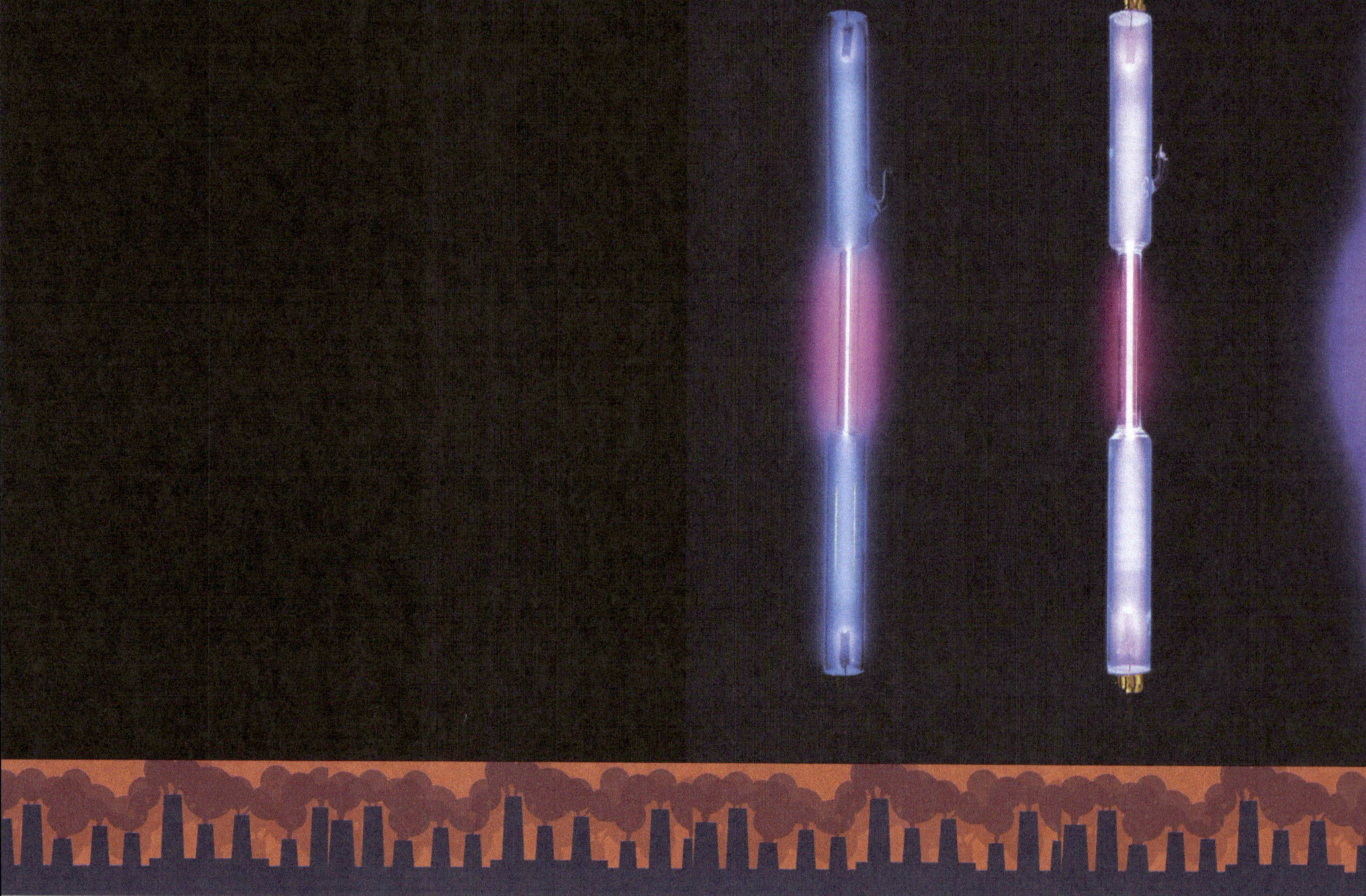

For a while scientists tried calling this group of elements "inert gases", thinking they could not form compounds at all.

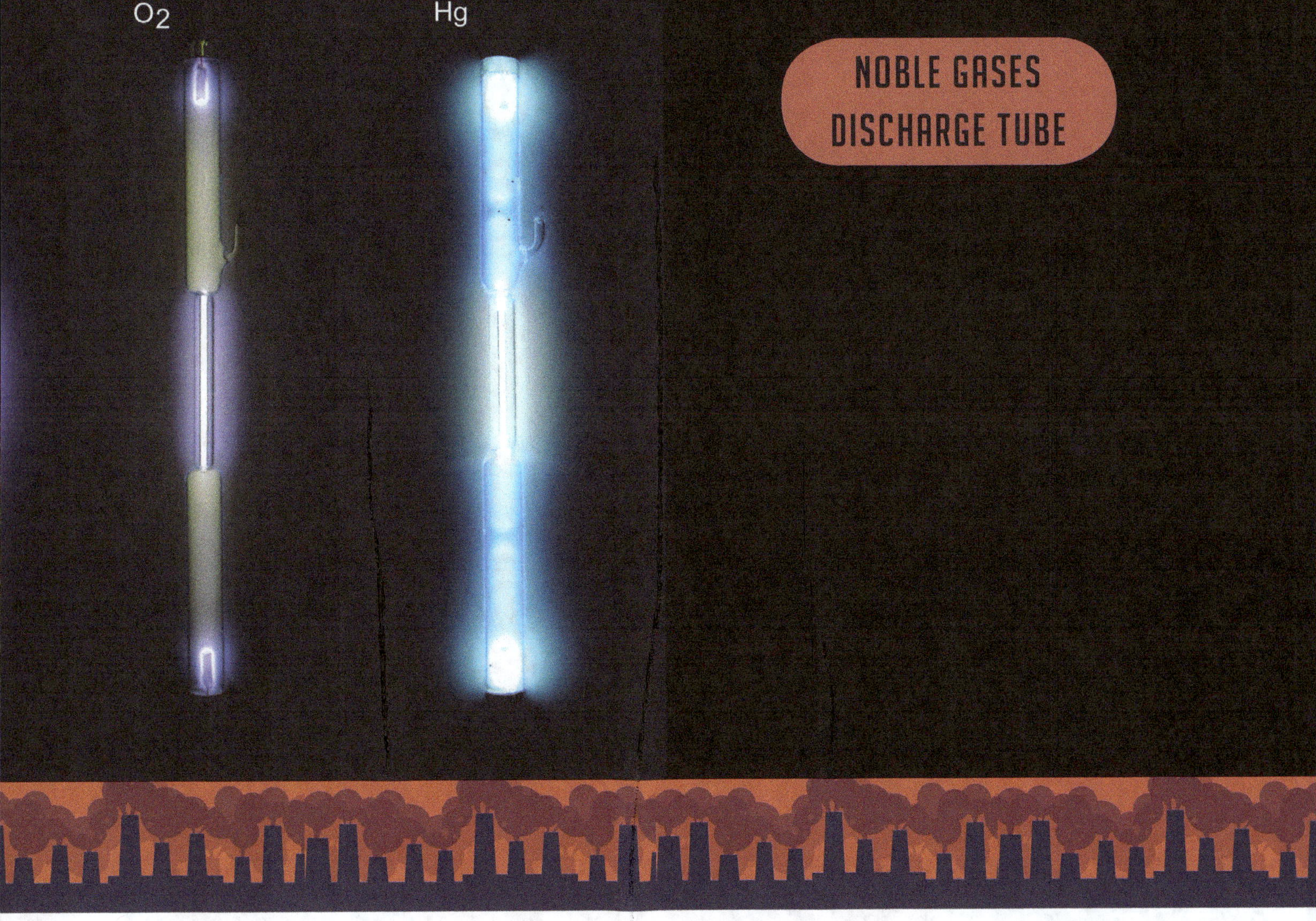

But once they started finding many noble gas compounds, the name did not seem accurate.

GAS TUBES FILLED WITH ARGON GAS

The noble gases make up a group at the far right side of the Periodic Table of the Elements.

The noble gases that exist in nature are:

- Helium (He)
- Neon (Ne)
- Argon (Ar)
- Krypton (Kr)
- Xenon (Xe)
- Radon (Rn)

Scientists have managed to create a single atom of oganesson (Og), and predict that it is a noble gas, but they are still trying to understand its properties.

118
Og
Oganesson
(294)

NOBLE GASES IN AN OUTDOOR STUDY

WHAT NOBLE GASES ARE LIKE

Noble gases share some features.

- They are colorless gases with no smell.
- Their melting and boiling points are very low and very close together, so they can be liquids only in very rare conditions.

Their atomic structure is stable: all of the noble gases except helium have eight electrons in their outer shell. This gives the atom a stable structure so it is less likely to form a compound with atoms of other elements. In fact, this gives the noble gases their other name: the "happy gases". This means they are happy to stay just the way they are, without combining with other elements.

COMPRESSED NATURAL HELIUM GAS
NON-FLAMMABLE GAS 2
HELIUM
UN 1046
NET WEIGHT
20 KG
FOR INDUSTRIAL USE ONLY
NON-FLAMMABLE GAS 2
HELIUM
UN 1046
NET WEIGHT
25 KG
FOR INDUSTRIAL USE ONLY
NON-FLAMMABLE GAS 2
HELIUM
UN 1046
NET WEIGHT
10 KG
FOR INDUSTRIAL USE ONLY
HELIUM
UN 1046
NET WEIGHT
6 KG
HELIUM
NET WEIGHT
8 KG

STRUCTURE OF XENON

They are the only "monatomic" elements. This means each molecule of a noble gas is a single atom, not a chain or collection of atoms of the element.

They are very rare in nature on Earth, although helium makes a large part of each star.

They were not discovered until the very end of the 19th century.

DISCOVERING THE NOBLE GASES

As early as 1784, chemist Henry Cavendish had noticed that air contains a small amount of something that is much less reactive than nitrogen. A hundred years later, Professor William Ramsay and Lord Rayleigh noticed that nitrogen samples taken from air had a different density than nitrogen that resulted from chemical reactions. That led them to the theory that nitrogen in the air was some-how mixed with another element.

HENRY CAVENDISH

HELIUM

After much work they isolated the new element, which they found very stable and not likely to form compounds. They called it "argon", after the Greek word for "lazy"!

In 1868 two scientists, Pierre Janssen and Joseph Norman Lockyer, discovered a new element in the Sun. They named it "helium" after the Greek word for "sun". Professor Ramsay later discovered helium on Earth while trying to isolate argon.

Helium and argon became the first members of a new section of the Periodic Table of the Elements!

Professor Ramsay continued experiments with air made so cold that it was a liquid rather than a gas. He was able to separate liquid air into the compounds and elements that are part of it. In 1898 he found three more elements:

- Krypton, from the Greek word for "hidden"

- Neon, from the Greek word for "new"

- Xenon, from the Greek word for "stranger"

PROFESSOR WILLIAM RAMSAY

LORD RAYLEIGH

Ramsay and Rayleigh won Nobel Prizes in physics and chemistry in 1904 for these discoveries. Finding a whole new group of elements had never been done before!

Friedrich Ernst Dorn identified radon in 1898 as a "radium emission", a gas resulting from radioactive decay of radium. By 1904 scientists came to understand that radon was part of the family of noble gases.

The noble gases occur in nature, or get created as a result of other processes. For instance, most of the helium in the universe was created at the "Big Bang",

the name scientists give for the huge event when the whole universe began. Helium is the most common element in the universe after hydrogen!

CONTAINER WITH LIQUID HELIUM

Most helium exists in stars, though, and it is much more rare on Earth. The other noble gases occur in small amounts in our atmosphere and in the ground, and get released during the breakdown of some compounds. Radon is released by the decay of some radioactive elements.

Trying to figure out why noble gases don't form compounds very easily helped scientists understand more about the structure of atoms. The Danish scientist Niels Bohr suggested in 1913, based on work with noble gases, that the electrons in atoms don't whiz around like tiny planets around a little sun (the nucleus of the atom). Instead, the electrons exist in "shells", or layers.

NIELS BOHR

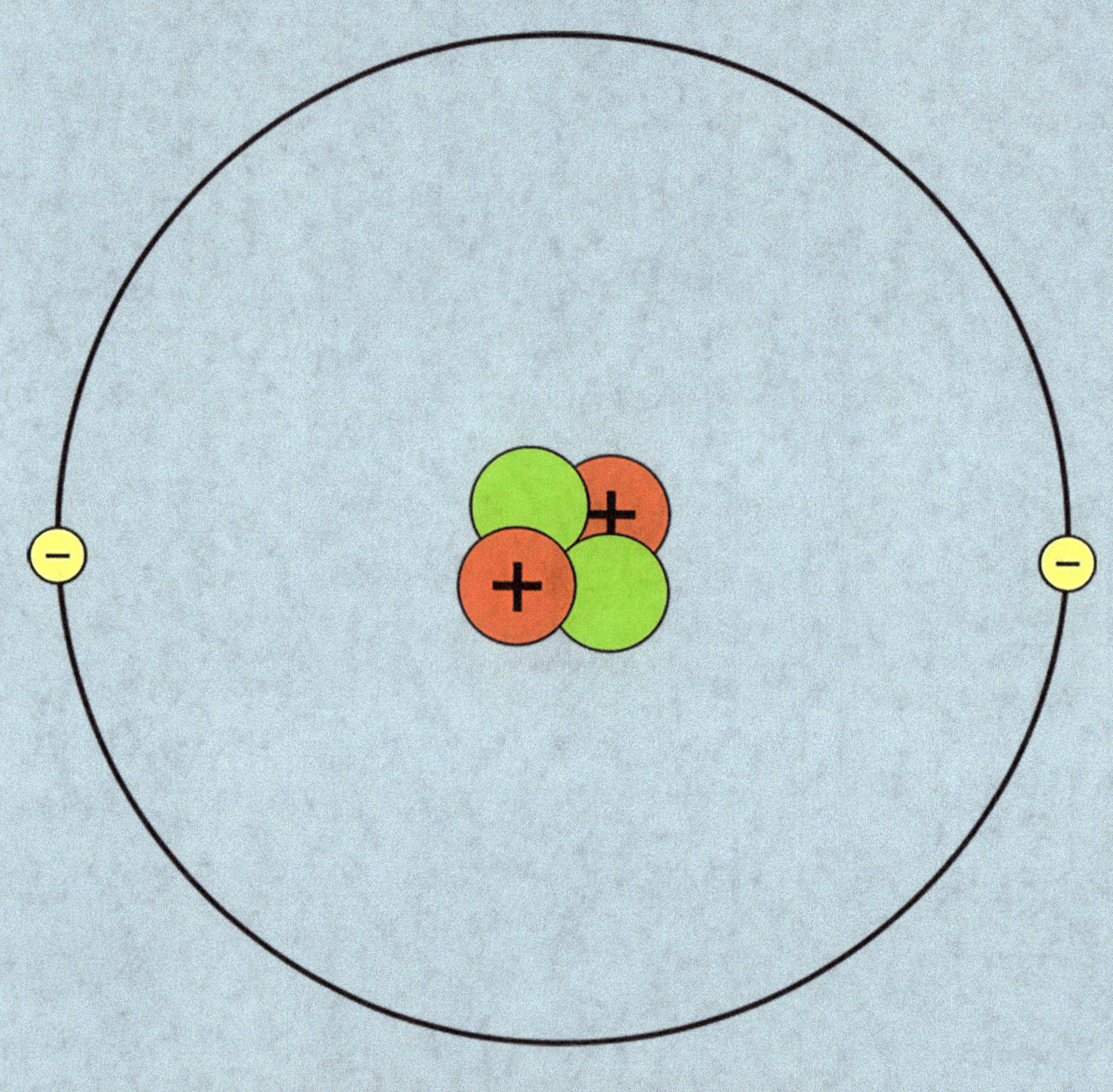

BOHR MODEL HELIUM ELEMENT

ohr suggested that the outside shell of the atom of a noble gas is very stable, as the outside shell of all of them except helium has eight electrons. In 1916 Gilbert Lewis proposed the "octet rule": any atom with an outer shell of eight electrons does not need more electrons to complete the shell, so it will not react easily with other elements in order to get more electrons.

It wasn't until 1962 that scientists identified stable chemical compounds involving noble gases. Recreating these compounds in laboratories usually involves very high temperatures and "bombarding" atoms of a noble gas with atoms of elements like calcium or fluorine.

Argon

Atomic number: 18
Atomic weight: 39.948
Per shell: 2, 8, 8

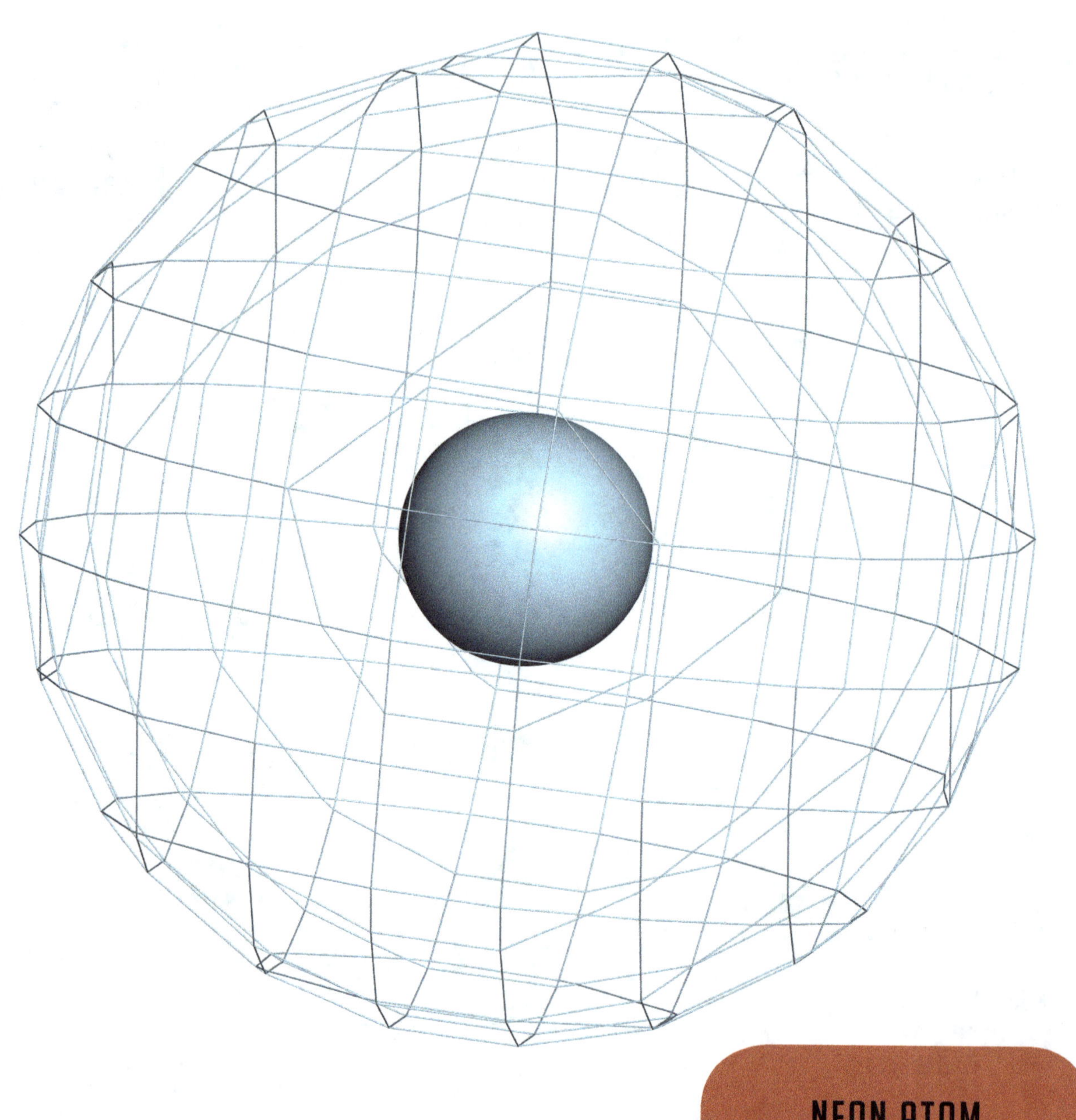

NEON ATOM

Of the noble gases, only helium and neon are actually inert and do not form compounds with other elements.

NOBLE AND USEFUL

The special properties of the noble gases mean they actually help in chemical research and in creating products for general use.

NON-FLAMMABLE GAS
2
ARGON
UN 1006
NET WEIGHT
20 KG
FOR INDUSTRIAL USE ONLY
NON-FLAMMABLE GAS
2
ARGON
UN 1006
NET WEIGHT
25 KG
FOR INDUSTRIAL USE ONLY
NON-FLAMMABLE GAS
2
ARGON
UN 1006
NET WEIGHT
10 KG
FOR INDUSTRIAL USE ONLY
ARGON
UN 1006
NET WEIGHT
6 KG
ARGON
UN 1006
NET WEIGHT
8 KG

ARGON ICE

Because the noble gases do not easily react with other elements, scientists use them to stabilize reactions in the laboratory that otherwise would happen too quickly for the scientists to study.

Noble gases boil and melt at very low temperatures. This means that, if you can make a noble gas so cold that it is a liquid, it will keep other things very cold. This is important in many laboratory processes.

LIGHT!

Makers of light bulbs often fill the bulb with argon to keep the hot filament from oxidizing (reacting with oxygen).

To make very bright lights, you can pass an electric charge through a container of krypton or xenon. Photographers use this to have strong light in their work...and so do lighthouse keepers! The headlights of cars often are filled with xenon gas because it, when an electric current passes through it, generates a light very much like daylight.

You may sometimes see glowing signs in the windows of stores or restaurants. The words are made with hollow glass tubes, and in the tubes there is often neon, which glows bright red when an electric charge passes through it. If you add some other compounds to the contents of the tube, you can get other colors.

A B C D E F G
H I J K L M N
O P Q R S T U
V W X Y Z ! ?
GLOWING NEON LIGHT

DEEP BREATHING

When deep-sea divers go down into the ocean, the increased pressure can change the air they are breathing and make them sick. To prevent the divers from getting "the bends", they breathe oxygen that has an increased amount of helium.

HIGH FLYING

You may have seen blimps, huge, long balloons that are so large that they can carry people and cargo under them. The first blimps, "dirigibles", were filled with hydrogen. Hydrogen does a very good job of lifting, as it is lighter than air, but it also burns. There were some terrible disasters with dirigibles crashing and burning. Blimps now use helium to hold them up, as part of its being an inert noble gas means that it does not burn.

Helium also fills weather balloons and inflates the large tires of jet planes because, in both cases, there is no risk of helium burning if there is an accident.

NOBLE MEDICINE

The noble gases play many roles in medicine:

- An MRI machine can scan the patient's body to understand what is going on in it. MRI machines use liquid helium to keep its superconducting magnets cool.

- For people who have trouble breathing because of a condition like asthma, adding some helium to their air supply can sometimes make it easier to breathe.

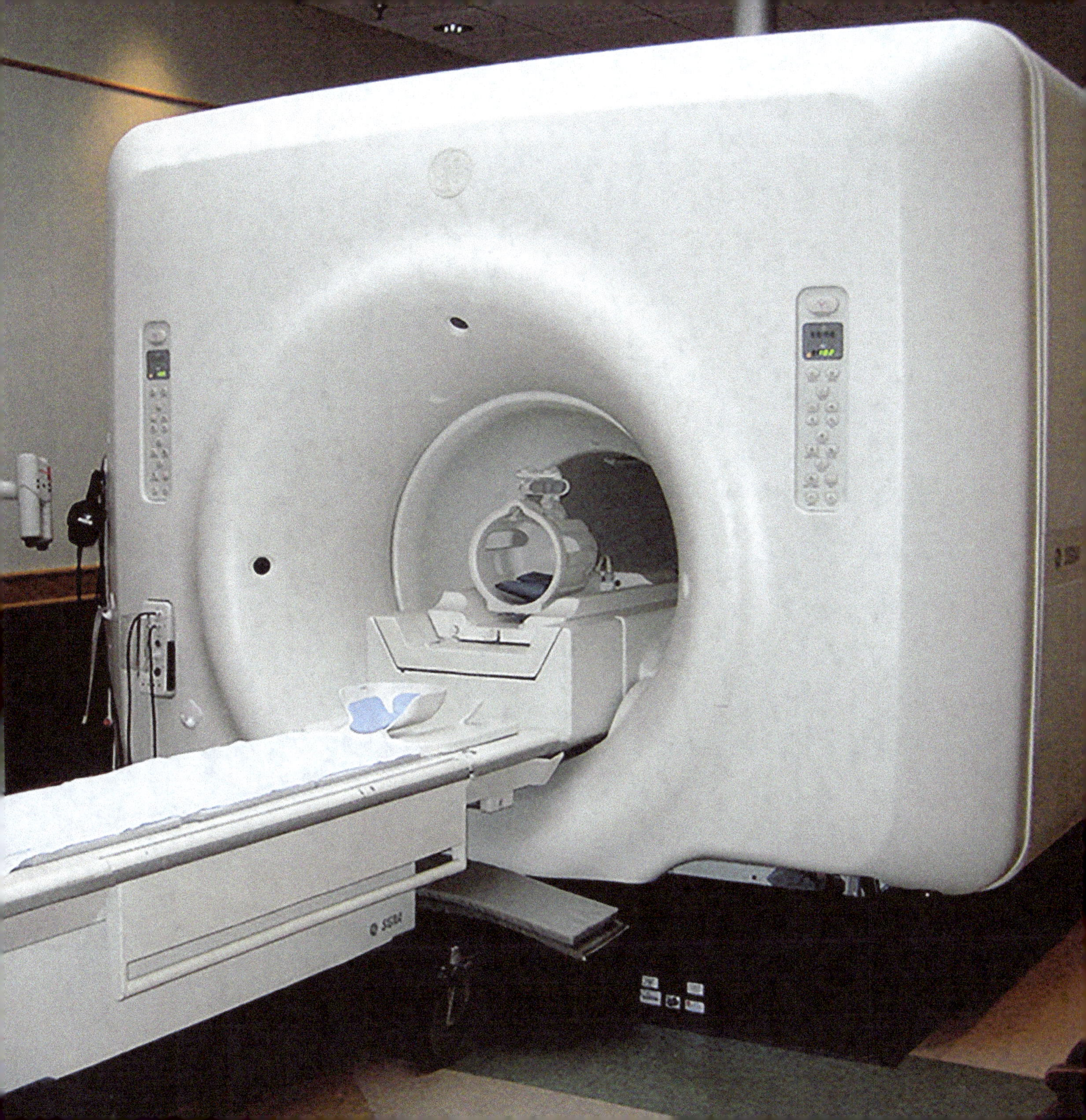

86
Rn
Radon
(222)

Xenon makes up part of general anaesthetics, partly because it dissolves quickly in the body and partly because the body gets rid of it quickly when the operation is over.

Radon is highly radioactive, which in general is not a good thing. However, very tiny amounts of radon can be used in radiotherapy, to treat certain illnesses.

SCIENTISTS EXPLORE THE WORLD

Understanding how our world works helps us live in it better. We can make better use of what our Earth offers while taking better care of it at the same time. Read Baby Professor books like Speed, Velocity, and Acceleration and What is Organic Chemistry? to grow your scientific knowledge.

Visit

BABY PROFESSOR
EDUCATION KIDS

www.BabyProfessorBooks.com

to download Free Baby Professor eBooks and view
our catalog of new and exciting Children's Books